PRE-SCHOOL THINKING SKILLS

Fun-filled Activities

An imprint of Om Books International

Same or Different

Tim and Tin are twins. Can you identify them? Circle (O) the two tortoises that are the same.

Same or Different

Help Cheeky, the mouse, find four balls that are different in the group.

Same or Different

Identify the same pictures in each group. Put a tick (✓) on the picture in each row that is the same as the first one.

Same or Different

Cross out (×) the picture in each row that is different from the rest of the group.

Matching

Draw lines to match the pictures on the left to the correct ones on the right.

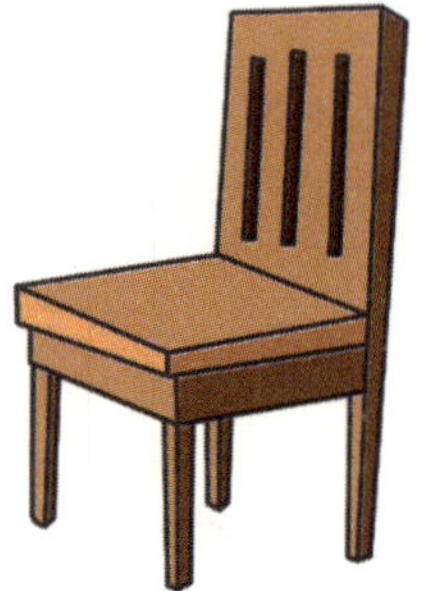

Matching

Can you match the left shoe with the right one? Let's try it out!

Matching

Draw lines from the animals to their food.

Classifying

Cross out (×) the one that does not fit in each group.

Classifying

Put a tick (✓) on the picture that does not belong in each group.

Classifying

Lee is out to buy fruits. Circle (O) all the shelves that have fruits and help him.

Classifying

Cross (×) out all the things that do not belong in the picture.

Grouping

Draw lines from the objects to the right basket.

Grouping

Circle (O) the things that belong in the sky.

Circle (O) the things that belong in the water.

Grouping

Circle (O) all the things that you find in the kitchen.

Grouping

The store is all messed up. Can you find and circle (O) all the articles of clothing from the store?

Sequencing

Tick (✓) the picture that shows what happened FIRST.

Sequencing

Circle (O) the picture that shows what happened NEXT.

1. First

2. First

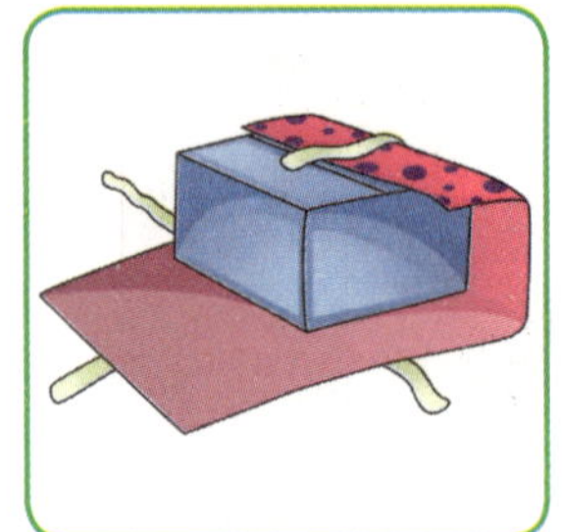

3. First

Sequencing

These pictures are not in order. To put them in order, write 1, 2 and 3 under each picture.

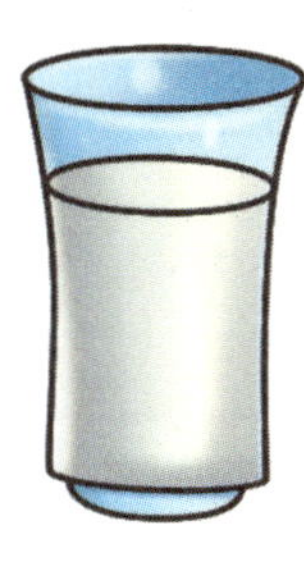

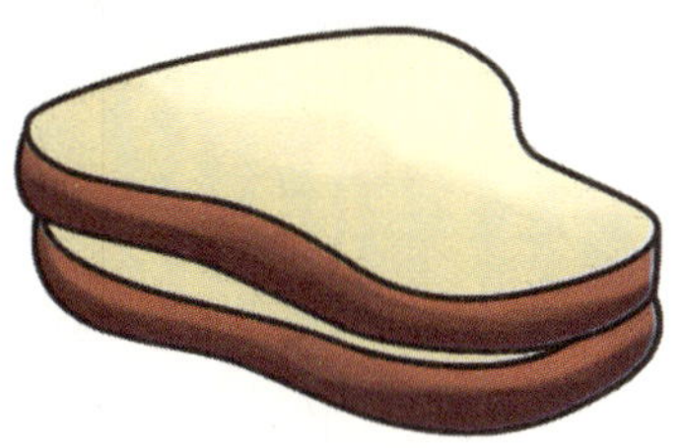
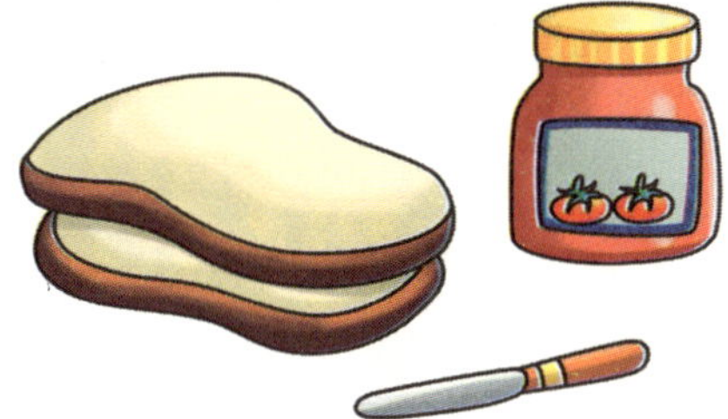

Sequencing

We do everything in a certain order. Write 1-4 so that the pictures are in the right order.

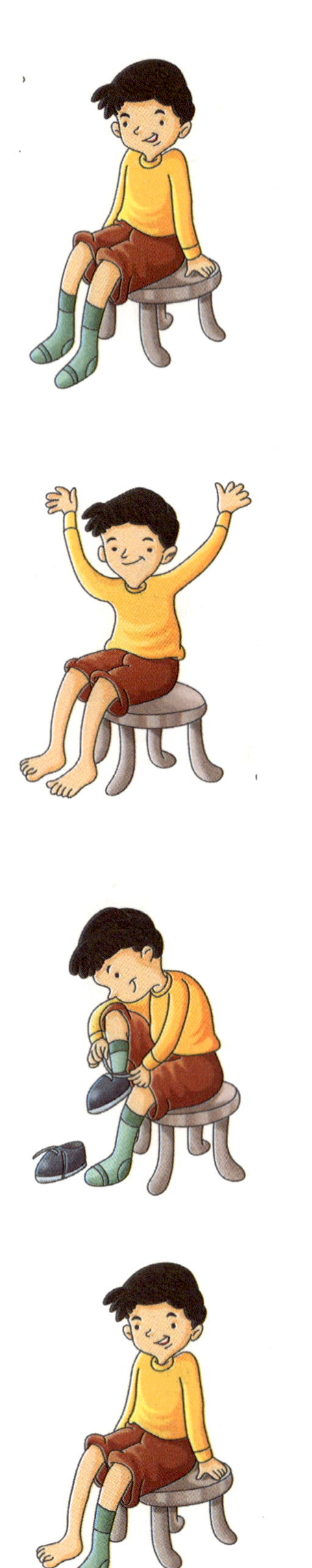

Observation

Bumpy, the bear is busy eating honey. Can you find and circle (O) its correct shadow? Try it out!

Observation

Can you find these hidden objects in the picture below? Circle (O) them.

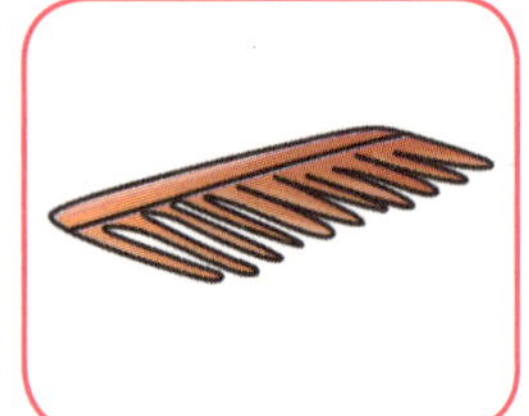

Observation

Find 8 differences between the two pictures given below.

Observation

Circle (O) the things that are wrong in the picture.

Following Directions

Directions:

1. Colour the umbrella green.
2. Colour the butterflies then the caterpillar.
3. Colour the shirt red.
4. Colour all big flowers pink.
5. Colour the 2 small flowers red.
6. Colour the rest of the picture the way you like.

Following Directions

Tick (✓) all the children who are inside the shoe house.

Circle (O) all the children that are outside.

Cross (×) all the animals that are on the car.

Draw one more ball near the cat.

Following Directions

Draw 2 buckets near the girl.

Draw 1 ball near the boy.

Draw 1 flag on the sandcastle.

Logical Thinking

Circle (O) the picture that comes next.

Logical Thinking

Read the clues below to find Ronny's bicycle. Cross (X) all the bicycles that do not fit the description. Circle (O) the correct bicycle.

Here are the clues:
The bicycle has a bell.
The bicycle is blue.
The bicycle has a flat tyre.

Logical Thinking

Who did it? Tick (✓) picture that shows who did it.

Answer Key

Page 2

Page 3

Page 4

Page 5

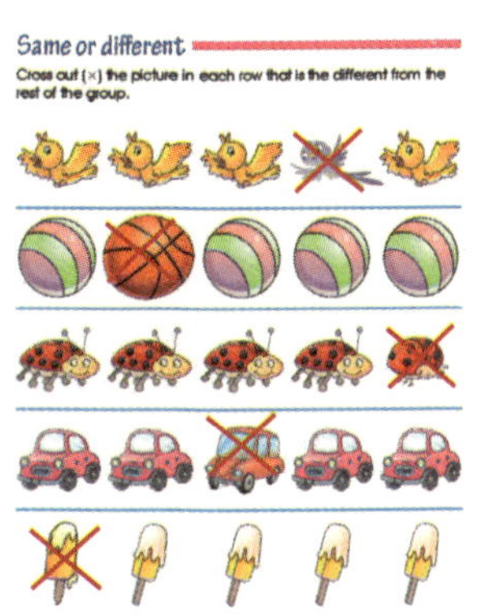

Page 6

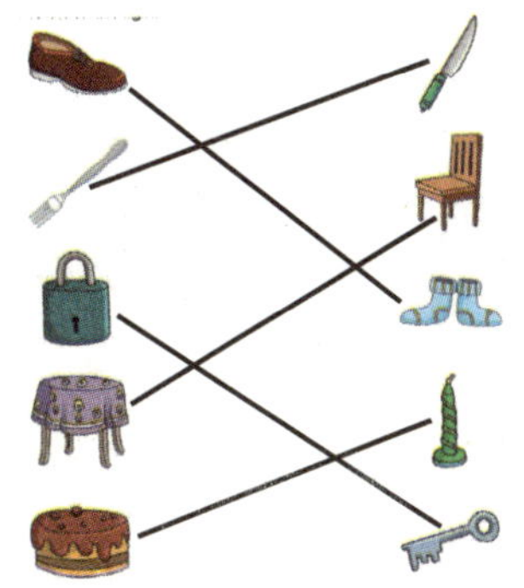

Page 7

Page 8

Page 9

Page 10

Page 11

Page 12

Page 13

Page 14

Page 15

Page 16

Page 17

Answer Key

Page 18

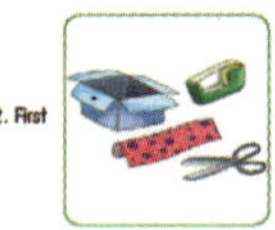

Page 19

Page 20

Page 21

Page 22

Page 23

Page 24

Page 25
Children will do on their own.

Page 26

Page 27
Children will do on their own.

Page 28

Page 29

Page 30

Answer Key

Page 2

Page 7

Page 12

Page 3

Page 8

Page 13

Page 4

Page 9

Page 14

Page 5

Page 10

Page 15

Page 6

Page 11

Page 16

Children will do on their own.

Page 17

Page 18

Page 19

Page 20

Page 21

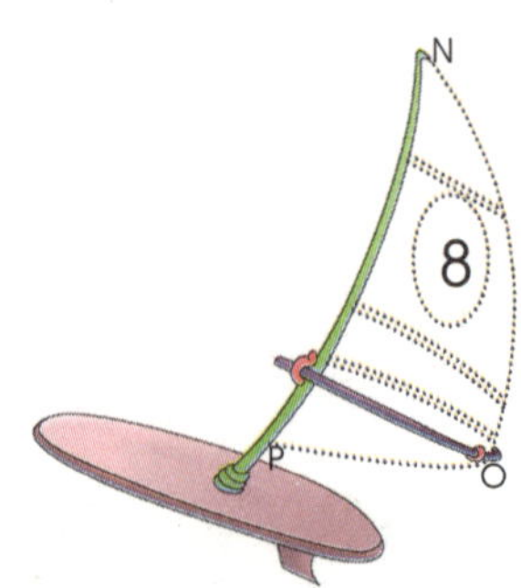

Page 22

Page 23

Page 24

Page 25

Page 26

Page 27

Page 28

Page 29

Page 30